LaDo

CHAOS of MIRACLES

BOOKS BY THE OSBORNS

BELIEVERS IN ACTION—*Apostolic–Rejuvenating*

BIBLICAL HEALING—*Seven Miracle Keys*
4 Visions–60+ yrs. of Proof–324 Merged Bible Vs.

FIVE CHOICES FOR WOMEN WHO WIN
21st Century Options

GOD'S BIG PICTURE—*An Impelling Gospel Classic*

GOD'S LOVE PLAN—*The Awesome Discovery*

HEALING THE SICK—*A Living Classic*

JESUS & WOMEN—*Big Questions Answered*

LIFE–TRIUMPH OVER TRAGEDY (WHY)
A True Story of Life After Death

MIRACLES-PROOF of God's Love

NEW LIFE FOR WOMEN—*Reality Refocused*

NEW MIRACLE LIFE NOW—*For Asia and The World*
Global Communiqué of The Christian Faith

PEACE *IS A LIFESTYLE*— *Truths for Crisis Times*

SOULWINNING—*Outside The Sanctuary*
A Classic on Biblical Christianity & Human Dignity

THE BEST OF LIFE—*Seven Energizing Dynamics*

THE GOOD LIFE—*A Mini-Bible School–1,467 Ref.*

THE GOSPEL ACCORDING TO T.L. & DAISY
Their Life & World Ministry–510 pg. Pictorial

THE MESSAGE THAT WORKS
T.L.'s Revealing Manifesto on Biblical Faith

THE POWER OF POSITIVE DESIRE
An Invigorating Faith Perspective

THE WOMAN BELIEVER—*Awareness of God's Design*

WOMAN WITHOUT LIMITS
Unmuzzled—Unfettered—Unimpeded

WOMEN & SELF-ESTEEM—*Divine Royalty Unrestrained*

YOU ARE GOD'S BEST—*Transforming Life Discoveries*

OSBORN Ministries International

USA HQ:

OSBORN MINISTRIES, INT'L

P.O. Box 10, Tulsa, OK 74102 USA

T.L. OSBORN, FOUNDER
LADONNA C. OSBORN, CEO

Tel: 918/743-6231
Fax: 918/749-0339   E-Mail: ministry@osborn.org
www.osborn.org

Canada: Box 281, Adelaide St. Post Sta., Toronto M5C 2J4
England: Box 148, Birmingham B3 2LG
(A Registered Charity)

BIBLE QUOTATIONS IN THIS BOOK MAY BE PERSONALIZED, PARAPHRASED, ABRIDGED OR CONFORMED TO THE *PERSON* AND *TENSE* OF THEIR CONTEXT IN ORDER TO FOSTER CLARITY AND INDIVIDUAL APPLICATION. VARIOUS LANGUAGE TRANSLATIONS AND VERSIONS HAVE BEEN CONSIDERED. BIBLICAL REFERENCES ENABLE THE READER TO COMPARE THE PASSAGES WITH HIS OR HER OWN BIBLE.

THE AUTHOR

ISBN 978-0-87943-185-3
Copyright 2011 by LaDonna C. Osborn
Printed in USA 2011-12
All Rights Reserved

Contents

Dr. LaDonna C. Osborn

Introduction
By Dr. T. L. Osborn

THE DEMOCRATIC REPUBLIC of the Congo (DRC) is a nation in tremendous conflict, and the 71 million people who live there are in desperate need of Christ's healing-love and His saving power.

The DRC, formerly known as Zaire, is the second largest country on the continent of Africa. Since 1998 ongoing internal lethal conflict has taken the lives of over 3.9 million Congolese (the deadliest war since World War II). Brutal attacks continue on the local populations including looting, rape, mutilations and murders. In the midst of such civic turmoil, economic crises and political corruption, the Christian believers struggle to deal with the overwhelming needs all around them.

The pastors and church leaders in the city of Kikwit pleaded with my daughter, Dr. LaDonna Osborn to come and bring a Gospel testimony to their city of over 300,000. Many of them remember the tremendous mass miracle crusades that my wife, Daisy, and I conducted in the cities of Kinshasa and Lubumbashi beginning in the late 1960's. The young generation has heard many stories from their parents and grandparents of what God did through our ministry in their country during that time.

Now they need to witness the miracles and experience the power of Christ for themselves. So Dr. LaDonna made the commitment to go to the DRC and to conduct a great *Osborn Gospel Seminar* and a public evangelism *Festival of Faith and Miracles*, in the city of Kikwit. After more than one year of planning, she assembled her team, and departed on this evangelism mission to bring the HOPE and HEALING of Jesus to this province of the Democratic Republic of the Congo.

In CHAOS OF MIRACLES Dr. LaDonna presents her day to day witness of God's great power during this historic and supernatural visitation of Christ to the DRC. You will experience the utter pandemonium that occurs when the miracle power of Jesus Christ sweeps over the multitudes that gather on a football field in this interior city of Kikwit.

Kinshasa (above) and Lubumbashi (below), the scene of tremendous mass miracle crusades conducted by the Osborns in the late 1960's.

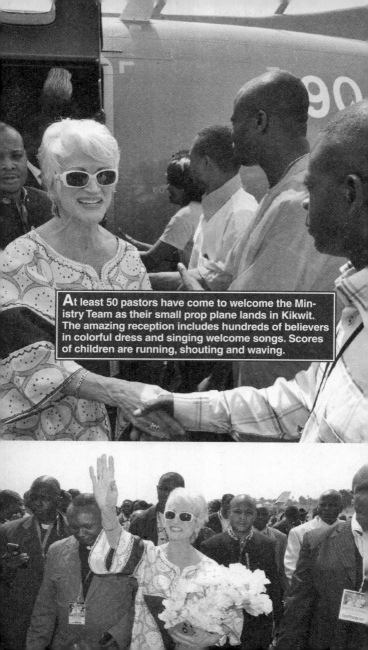

At least 50 pastors have come to welcome the Ministry Team as their small prop plane lands in Kikwit. The amazing reception includes hundreds of believers in colorful dress and singing welcome songs. Scores of children are running, shouting and waving.

Chapter I

Return To Africa

WE ARRIVE IN Kinshasa, Democratic Republic of the Congo just as the sun is setting against the beautiful African sky. A unique joy always accompanies me when I return "home" to Africa.

As I climb into the shuttle bus that will transport us from the airplane to "Arrivals," a suffocating heat announces that I am once again in the equatorial tropics.

New Visitation for New Generation

A new generation of young people is rising in the Democratic Republic of the Congo, formerly known as Zaire. Many things have not changed in this country since my parents conducted tremendous and historic miracle evangelism crusades here in the late 60's and early 70's.

But this new generation is eager to learn about the powerful Gospel of Christ and to see Jesus' miracle wonders. Their parents have told them many stories about what God did when my parents came to Kinshasa and Lubumbashi many years ago. *Therefore you shall lay up these words of mine in your heart and in your soul... You shall teach them to your children, speaking of them when you sit in your house, when you walk by the way, when you lie down, and when you rise up.*[Deut. 11:18-19 NKJV] Now they are determined to witness the miracles and experience the presence of Christ for themselves.

Pastors' Involvement is Vital

After the snail-paced process through immigration, 12 beautiful Kinshasa pastors greet me. They are smiling and beaming with hands eager to touch me and to express their warm welcome. We have been diligently working with these men and women of God for nearly one year, preparing for the national *Osborn Gospel Seminar* for pastors, church leaders and Christian believers, and the four-day public evangelism *Festival of Faith and Miracles* where tens of thousands of Congolese will accept Jesus Christ as their Lord and Savior.

While sitting in the tiny airport waiting room, I visit with the leading host pastor and my interpreter. They give me updates on issues at hand and on the challenges that await me in Kikwit. These reports come as no surprise to me, for there are always obstacles to doing the work of God. But we are always victorious. *Always!*

...thanks be to God, who gives us the victory through our Lord Jesus Christ.
1Cor. 15:57 NKJV

God is Our Faithful Provider

My luggage is finally located, and I am escorted to a lovely vehicle that is being provided by one of the Kinshasa pastors. I'm touched to learn that he is paying $150 per day to provide this transportation convenience and air-conditioned comfort. After several miles of skillful maneuvering around buses, people and potholes, we arrive at our hotel, which is intentionally hidden behind a walled compound.

I remember this place from our previous mission to DRC. After the final Festival day in Matadi, my team and I traveled more than eight hours through the night as we returned to Kinshasa so we could make the connection with our international flight back to the United States. This very weary preacher welcomed the simple comforts offered by this Kinshasa hotel.

Now on my return to the DRC I

consider this hotel room my home away from home (as I always do) and I thank God for His provision. I am delighted to see that it has an air conditioning unit and convenient electrical outlets. I will wait here in Kinshasa until my mission team arrives, and then we will all journey together by air to Kikwit, thus avoiding the arduous 12-hour road trip.

A perfect dinner of rice and a green vegetable (somewhat like spinach) is brought to my room. After unpacking and waiting for the water to be turned on, I bathe and lay on the bed, ready for a much needed and restful sleep. As though on cue for my pleasure, a soft rain begins to fall. The soothing sound of a tropical rain shower on the tin roofs is like therapy to this sleep-deprived traveler. Already at the very beginning of this mission, I am reminded of God's promise: ...*my God shall supply all your need according to His riches in glory by Christ Jesus.* Phil.4:19 NKJV Thank You Jesus!

Journey to Kikwit

After another day, my mission team joins me in Kinshasa. The team consists of Reverend Harry Jackson, my Global Ministry Coordinator, Reverend Jennifer Yeager, our video photographer, and my grandson, Aaron Thomas, our still photographer. We feel that one of our vital responsibilities is to document the great wonders that are performed by Christ among people of this 21st Century so that we will *remember well what the Lord...did.* Deut.7:18 NKJV Our Gospel books and ministry reports always include pictures, to testify of the faithfulness of Christ in this generation.

Prior to boarding the plane for the flight to Kikwit, we are required to pay for excess baggage weight due to our heavy batteries and video equipment. Additionally, we are charged an airport tax and a fee for using the VIP waiting room, a total of over $400! Nothing is cheap in this ministry of world evangelism, even with our extensive cost-saving efforts.

Once our aircraft is airborne, the flight over the jungle to Kikwit is uneventful. Looking down from the small plane to the trees and villages below, I reflect on the many such flights that I've experienced in my life. From the age of ten months, my life has been filled with journeys, by prop plane, by boat and overland, traveling with my courageous pioneering parents as they forged the evangelism trails that I follow today.

Amazing Reception in Kikwit

After an hour and a half in the small 12-seat prop plane, we land in Kikwit where we receive one of the most amazing welcomes that I've experienced in recent years. At least 50 pastors have come to welcome our team. Hundreds of believers in colorful dress are singing welcome songs. Scores of children are running, shouting and waving.

In Kikwit there are no airport immigration formalities. So after an impromptu interview with a reporter from the local radio station, I am escorted to a vehicle with an open top. The host pastor requests that I stand up in the vehicle so that the people can see me as we drive into the city. It is estimated that tens of thousands of people have lined the 10-kilometer road from the airport into Kikwit. The excitement is contagious. Old and young people alike are waving their hands and smiling. They shout, "Welcome Bishop LaDonna, servant of God. He has heard our prayers and now we see you with our own eyes."

A parade consisting of over a dozen cars and hundreds of motorcycles escorts us into the city, all while I continue to stand up through the vehicle's open top, waving to the people with my hair blowing in the wind. It is a joyful sight to see the excitement on the faces of the people, knowing that even their highest expectations will be far surpassed by the loving power of Christ.

"Home" Away From Home

"You are in the countryside," is the explanation I'm given for the inconveniences that our hotel imposes. Having no running water is not a problem, as buckets of water are generously provided and gasoline generators provide electricity for five hours daily, from 6 to 11 p.m. The heat is sweltering but we dare not open the windows due to the swarms of mosquitoes in this area of DRC.

Sleeping under mosquito nets is not a new experience for me. Some of my earliest childhood memories are of our family "creating home" wherever we were around the world, as we considered sleeping cots and mosquito nets to be normal fixtures in our "homes." I thank God for my heritage of world ministry, which has uniquely prepared me for the missions on which Christ sends me today.

The hotel management informs us that if we will pay an additional $144 per day for gasoline and engine oil, for the generators, we will be provided with electricity from midnight until 8 a.m. Of course that would be wonderful, but we will be here for 17 days, and we simply cannot afford the extra $2448 for electricity. After many hours of diplomatic negotiation, I have been able to arrange for two additional hours of electricity daily, from 6 a.m. to 8 a.m. for a small fee. This will be a tremendous help that will provide us with light, power and air conditioning, as we prepare for each day's ministry. This is a huge blessing at a small expense.

A parade consisting of over a dozen cars and hundreds of motorcycles welcomes Bishop LaDonna to Kikwit (see photo spread, next page). Throngs of people line the street, shouting "Welcome Bishop LaDonna, servant of God. He has heard our prayers and now we see you with our own eyes."

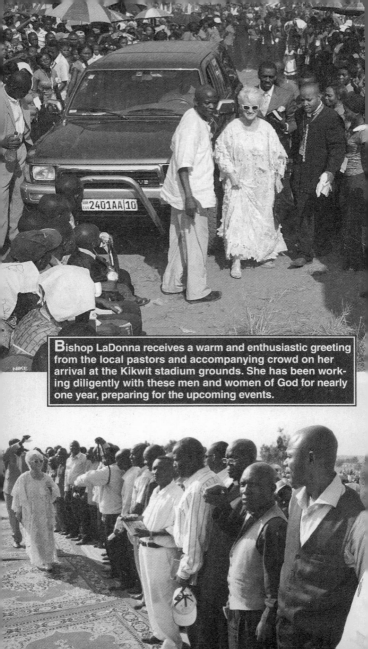

Bishop LaDonna receives a warm and enthusiastic greeting from the local pastors and accompanying crowd on her arrival at the Kikwit stadium grounds. She has been working diligently with these men and women of God for nearly one year, preparing for the upcoming events.

Chapter 2

Gospel Seminar
Impacts Believers

IT IS IMPRESSIVE to see that the people are gathering at the seminar venue by 7 a.m. each morning. These dear people have arrived hours prior to the starting time of the first session, and many have traveled great distances to come and experience what God is doing in Kikwit. By 8:30 a.m. the daily sessions begin, and they continue until 5 or 5:30 p.m. each evening.

I convene the *Osborn Gospel Seminar* in the only building in Kikwit that is large enough for this event. The main room is packed with over 2,000 people and hundreds of more listeners fill another room that is located behind a balcony wall. Those in this room cannot see, but they are satisfied to be able to hear the teaching.

Unite–Prepare–Mobilize

The purpose of this seminar is to unite the pastors of many different denominations around the central message of Christ, and to instill in the Christian community of Kikwit an understanding that evangelism is the primary task of the Church. During the seminar I am also preparing the pastors and believers for the upcoming public evangelism *Festival of Faith and Miracles* and mobilizing every Christian as a representative of Christ in their own communities.

During the first session I begin by carefully laying the foundation for *all* biblical truth. This foundation is the one story of the Bible, the story of God and His plan for humankind, made in His image. This one story–that begins in Genesis and continues through the Scriptures–is the Gospel, the Good News.

When believers understand the foundational truths of the Gospel, they easily receive the knowledge that is necessary for them to discern the truths of God's Word. It is apparent to these Congolese believers that the Lord is speaking to them through me.

**Tradition bows to
the supremacy of truth.**

**The powerful Gospel story
shatters the yokes of bondage
and sets people free.**

The Lord is strategically guiding the instruction through each session of this great *Osborn Gospel Seminar*. He loves His people so much, and He wants them to know Him as a God of mercy and truth. I am always amazed at the uniqueness of how He speaks through me to people in so many various cultures. This is the work of the Holy Spirit, who empowers us to be effective communicators of the message of Christ.

No one leaves. Not one single person! They are listening to me very carefully, and they are embracing each truth and every concept that I am revealing to them from the Scripture. Occasionally throughout the teaching, the people jump to their feet, and begin rejoicing and praising God for His great love and for His amazing plan for all humankind. I have no choice but to pause, and rejoice with them.

Osborn Partners Are Valued

I thank God for sending us to Kikwit, even though the circumstances here are not easy. Everything is very expensive. As I mentioned previously, in order for us to have electricity provided in our hotel rooms, we must pay for the gasoline and engine oil to keep the generators running. Even after negotiations, the cost is nearly $25 for each hour that we receive electricity for lights, for the small window air conditioner, and for recharging our camera and computer batteries. So we endure the heat, paying the fees for only the few hours daily when electricity is needed most.

Right now I'm sitting in a dark room, documenting our mission on my iPhone so that I may share these details with you. This mission is only possible because of our friends and partners who plant their mission seeds in this ministry to hurting people. We thank God for each one. Yet we're also praying that God will call more believers to partner with us so that we may conduct these vital missions without these financial limitations.

We have not been able to print sufficient books for distribution here in Kikwit. The need is so great. But we thank God for what we are able to do. We, along with our partners, are here as part of God's love-solution for the people of the Democratic Republic of the Congo!

Women in God's Plan

One session of the *Osborn Gospel Seminar* is purposefully dedicated to teaching the biblical position of redeemed women in God's Plan. These truths are desperately needed worldwide and especially in these nations where the female is considered to have little value. Their potential for the work of Christ is great, yet they struggle under the burdens of restrictive cultures and traditional, unbiblical teachings.

Beginning in the Book of Genesis, I reveal the details of God's original plan for people that include dignity, relationship and equality. As I carefully reveal each biblical truth layer by layer, the women jump up from their seats and begin waving their arms and shouting with joy as they see for themselves that the Scripture defines their rightful place in the plan of God.

There is a powerful strength among these Christian women that must be directed toward the ministry of Christ on earth, as His Body, the Church. These women are bold, and with faith in God and with the power of the Holy Spirit, they have the ability to bring about positive change in their nation.

This final Seminar day is filled with expectation. The venue is packed, and it is so hot. The air circulation is minimal because the door openings are filled with people from the surrounding market, pressing forward in an attempt to just catch a glimpse of what is going on.

After teaching on the necessity of MIRACLES in ministry to prove the resurrection life of Jesus to those who do not know Him, the pastors and believers are filled with excitement and faith to experience miracles in their own lives and in their own ministries. After each sentence I have to just stop and let them shout as the truth and its POWER explodes within them.

Gospel Books Planted in Kikwit

The books that will be distributed here in Kikwit have arrived overland by truck. As they are offloaded at the Seminar venue, I am aware of the great value of these books to the work of God in this region of Africa. Our partners cannot imagine the harvests that their seed-gifts will continue to reap in souls and in the lives of these Gospel-taught Congolese men and women.

There are literally three huge piles of our books on the floor in front of the platform. We are distributing NEW MIRACLE LIFE NOW, GOD'S BIG PICTURE and 10 GOSPEL BASICS. The truths in these Gospel materials will both transform the thinking of the church leaders and will help to ground the new converts in their redeemed status in Christ.

It is impossible to organize the book distribution as we usually do. The people are packed in every corner of the building. There are scarcely any aisles through which they can maneuver. I seize the opportunity and direct our photographer to capture a photographic sweep of the crowd before distributing the gift books. There is such joy on the faces of these beautiful people. Then we begin the distribution. In spite of every effort to create a smooth process for presenting the books, there is still much shouting and pushing as believers press forward to receive their gift. After an hour there are still about 1500 people waiting for their turn to receive their books.

There are no words to describe the people's desire for these materials, or to express their desperate need for the truths that these books contain.

I thank God that because of a few of our faithful partners who sacrifice to make these book distributions possible, we are able to plant these powerful seeds into the lives of these Congolese believers.

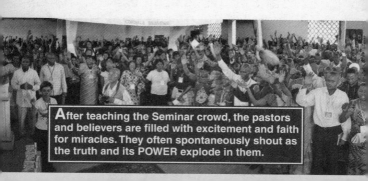

After teaching the Seminar crowd, the pastors and believers are filled with excitement and faith for miracles. They often spontaneously shout as the truth and its POWER explode in them.

There are no words to describe the people's desire for the three Osborn books in French, or to express their desperate need for the truths that these books contain.

GRANDE CONFERENCE DES SERVITEURS DE
AVEC
BISHOP LADONNA BORE
DES USA À KIKWIT

After the book distribution, Bishop LaDonna gathers all the pastors for a special meeting to prepare for the upcoming *Festival of Faith and Miracles*. This is the first time that all of the Kikwit pastors have worked together for a cooperative event.

A group of local business leaders listens intently as Bishop LaDonna shares with them about the sacrifices that faithful ministry partners have made to help finance this great Kikwit visitation. They respond enthusiastically with their support and participation.

Following the distribution of flyers advertising the Festival, Bishop LaDonna and her Ministry Team return to their hotel. As the car stops, they are unable to get out of the vehicle because of the press of people surrounding the car. The hunger is so great, it can be clearly seen why God sent them here to Kikwit.

Chapter 3

Focus Shifts to Evangelism

AFTER THE BOOK distribution, I gather all of the pastors for a special meeting. They have been working hard to prepare for these Gospel events and now they are beginning to reap the reward.

News of Seminar Success Spreads

The Pastors are excited because this is the first time that all of the Kikwit pastors have worked together for cooperative events. They are learning the power of unity as they witness what can be accomplished when many pastors join together to do something great for Christ in their town.

There are at least 250 pastors present. I share with them the details of the upcoming evangelism *Festival of Faith and Miracles*, and I also coach them on their strategic roles during this public soulwinning event. They are full of great expectation.

Testimonies and reports are pouring in after the completion of the *Osborn Gospel Seminar*. The pastors are saying:

"We have been preaching all that we knew. This woman of God has shown us things in the Bible that our eyes were blinded to.

"Now we see Jesus.

"Now we have respect for the women.

"Now we know the plan of God.

"Our city will never be the same.

"Dr. LaDonna has brought the light of Jesus and His truth to us."

It is evident that Christ and His truth have been received with great joy.

Inspiring Kikwit
Business Leaders

In just a few days the historic Gospel evangelism *Festival of Faith and Miracles* will begin. There has never been such an event conducted in Kikwit.

The venue for the Festival is a large open football field that is known by everyone. It is the perfect place where people can come and bring their sick and their lame to be healed by the loving POWER of Jesus. But first there is much preparation to be done.

The business people of Kikwit have invited me to come and speak to them at a special event organized for the purpose of informing the business community about the upcoming events that will impact their city. I love to help business people understand the high regard with which God esteems them as partners with Him in His program.

As I stand face-to-face with these 100 business owners, in an open-air café, it is obvious to me that they are eager to learn what the Bible teaches about God's desire to prosper people who do His good work.

After I show them God's plan to prosper His people, I teach them HOW to give. So often people are coerced into giving, or they give for the wrong reasons. It is wonderful to learn from the Scripture that giving is a cheerful, faith-filled and deliberate action.

I share with these business people about the sacrifices that our faithful ministry partners have made to help us finance this great Kikwit visitation. They are the ones who have provided for the printing of the thousands of books that have been distributed to the believers here. But I also communicate to them that we have come by faith, trusting in the Lord for everything that is needed to convene the upcoming *Festival of Faith and Miracles*, so that we may bring blessing to Kikwit.

After teaching them for about one hour, I pray for them as I continue standing in the middle of the courtyard surrounded by these beautiful businessmen and women. As I pray I ask God to show them how they can participate with God's program here by giving of their financial means. I pray that God will show them what to give that will be for the good of God, and for the good of the people here in Kikwit. It is wonderful to give people an opportunity to invest themselves (through their money) in God's love-mission to people.

Then I stand beside an old battered wooden table that is sitting in the middle of the courtyard, and I tell the people to come and lay their gifts before the Lord. Everyone starts moving, bringing his or her Congo Francs as an investment in the work of God. Most of the money is so tattered and worn. It isn't very attractive nor does it look valuable. But in the hands of God, this money will be converted into a *soul-harvest* of people who will make a difference in this nation. This is the most valuable of all investments!

I am confident that by the time we leave Kikwit, ALL of our financial needs for this mission will be met. *For with God nothing will be impossible.* Lu.1:37 NKJV

Christians Hit The Streets

Now is the time to mobilize the Christians of Kikwit by sending them out to every street, market, home and to the surrounding villages with special invitations for people to come to this great *Festival of Faith and Miracles.* Passionate and loving Christians are the key to any successful evangelism event. My goal is to make sure that these believers understand this important biblical principle.

At least 1,500 believers have packed into the one building large enough to hold the crowd. I begin by telling them that THEY are the ones who will guarantee the success of this soul-winning Festival that will bring blessing to their entire region. The commands of Jesus to His followers are read from the Scripture and the story of the Early Church is rehearsed, reminding them what happens when believers that are full of the Holy Spirit tell others about Jesus.

> **I remind them that the miracles of Jesus are what convince people that He is truly alive today.**

It is thrilling to see the excitement grow in the believers as they begin to realize that Jesus wants to do the same things through them that He did through His followers in Bible days.

> **Early Church ministry continues wherever there are people with Bible faith doing Bible actions.**

After about one hour of teaching, we distribute the printed invitations that the believers will present to the people of Kikwit. Each invitation includes strategic words of welcome and information, plus photographs of multitudes and of people who have previously been healed by the power of God. We pray and ask that the Lord will give each believer wisdom as they compel people to come to the Festival, bringing their sick and their lame.

Scores of young ushers assist me in distributing the invitations to the Christians who will in turn distribute them to everyone in the city and throughout the surrounding area. The people are so eager to let others know that the Healing Jesus is visiting Kikwit. The noise of the distribution drowns out everything else in the auditorium. People press forward to receive their portion of these beautiful invitations. They are so excited; no one wants to be left out.

These believers have come alive with the power and purpose of Christ. As I look over the crowd, I am touched by the simplicity of these village people who are so vital to the work of Christ.

**Truly Jesus has purposed
to do His mighty work
through ordinary people.**

After we pray and dismiss the people, the team and I are transported
by car back to our hotel. As we drive
along the road, we can see Festival
invitations already in the hands of
people throughout the town, all the
way to the front door of our hotel.
We are amazed! How did they get
here so fast?

When our car stops, we are unable
to get out of the vehicle because of the
press of people surrounding our car
who want to know more about the
Miracle Festival. The hunger is so
great. We can clearly see why God
sent us here to Kikwit.

**The harvest is ready to be reaped,
and we are ready for the task.**

After a few words of welcome, Dr. LaDonna prays, dedicating the grounds to the glory of God. Then she immediately begins teaching the people about the one true God of creation who loves them and who sent her to tell them that He wants to come to them with love and with miracle-solution for their many needs.

The people continue to arrive and pack into the Festival grounds, the crowd soon swelling to an estimated 80,000 attendees. Dr. LaDonna hardly finishes her message when miracles begin to break out among the excited crowd.

Chapter 4

Festival of Faith and Miracles Begins

AS I PREPARE to leave my hotel for the football field on the first day of this evangelism *Festival of Faith and Miracles*, I am told that the streets are lined with thousands of people who are coming to the field. I am confident that the people who come will witness a great display of Christ's loving power. As we proclaim His Gospel, Jesus will demonstrate His compassion and resurrection life here in Kikwit!

Words cannot describe what we are witnessing during this first historic Festival service. When my team and I arrive at the enormous venue, it is already filled with a multitude. It is estimated that 80,000 people are packed tightly together. The chairman of the Festival has not yet arrived so I open the Festival myself. Suffering people must not be kept waiting.

After a few words of welcome, I pray, dedicating the grounds to the glory of God and I pray for the nation of the Democratic Republic of the Congo.

Then I immediately begin teaching the people about the one true God of creation who loves them and who sent me to tell them that He wants to come to them with love and with miracle-solution for their many needs.

Only Jesus Has The Power to Forgive and Heal

The story of the paralytic in the Gospel of Luke, chapter 5, verses 18-25, helps the people to understand the divine power of Jesus. He alone has the power to forgive sins. He alone has the power to cure diseases.

By the time I teach the people how Jesus healed the paralytic, the people on one side of the crowd begin to shout. A crippled man has thrown down his crutches and he is walking. The energy of excitement flows through the people as they begin to realize what is happening. They shout and point and push to see the crippled man who is now walking without his crutches by the power of Jesus.

Gradually I am able to regain the attention of the multitude and lead them to the decision to believe on Jesus and to accept Him into their lives. It seems that all of the people are eager to receive Jesus and to be born again. After the prayer the multitude has been transformed into a sea of 80,000 smiling faces. After a lifetime of seeing such scenes around the world, it still takes my breath away when a multitude of people raises their hands and accepts Jesus as their Savior.

A Miracle Wind Blows in Kikwit

There is a swell of faith and excitement building in the atmosphere, so I do not take time to give special instructions to the new believers. Instead, I begin preparing the people for the healing prayer. I tell them to lay their hands on their sick bodies, just as I do during every Festival that we conduct all over the world.

But just before I start to pray, I look to my left and see a very strong wind stirring in the tops of the trees on one side of the field. The wind reaches the ground and begins to move toward the people. The trees that surround the field are bending in the wind and a cloud begins to settle over the people. They are shouting and they are pushing.

A little boy is already walking as his mother holds his crutch up in the air thanking Jesus. All through the multitude crutches are being raised into the air. Cripples are walking across the platform. Here comes the little boy with a bold look of determination on his face as he walks back and forth across the platform.

No healing prayer has been prayed, but the power of the Lord is present and *He is healing*!

I discover at least two blind people who have received their sight.

The platform is now completely filled with healed people and excited pastors. They are shouting with joy, and we cannot quiet them sufficiently so that we can hear the testimonies of those who have been healed. This *supernatural chaos* is the result of Christ's awesome miracle power at work among the people.

I often tell preachers, while I am preparing them for the Festival activities:

"It is impossible to organize the miraculous. We must always allow Christ to be Himself among His people."

This CHAOS OF MIRACLES is marvelous to behold; Bible days are being witnessed in Kikwit.

More crutches are being raised into the air. A wheelchair has been lifted above the multitude of people and it has now been placed on the platform. A large pile of crutches and walking sticks is materializing across the front of the platform.

During Day One of the *Festival of Faith and Miracles*, a very strong wind reaches the ground and begins to move toward the people. The trees that surround the field are bending in the wind and a cloud begins to settle over the people.

There is a swell of faith and excitement building during the first day of the *Festival of Faith and Miracles*. Dr. LaDonna tells the people to lay their hands on their sick bodies, just as she does during every Festival that is conducted all over the world.

Chapter 5

The Wonder of The Supernatural

BY THIS TIME it is apparent that I must close the meeting before a human stampede erupts. Desperate people are now trying to get to the platform. Those who are at the far edge of the crowd are pushing forward, thinking that the source for their miracle is with me. The pressure is like a human tidal wave that cannot be controlled.

The ushers are asked to give assistance to my team and me as we attempt to exit the grounds to prevent the multitude from pushing toward the platform. If we do not leave now, many people will certainly be injured. We must not allow that to happen.

I ask my interpreter to stay with the people and to encourage them to continue trusting God for the miracles that they need and to be careful to not step on the sick that are lying on the grounds. I also tell him to instruct the multitude to tell others what they have witnessed tonight and to return tomorrow, bringing those who are sick and diseased so that they may also receive their miracle. Tomorrow we will hear the reports of what God has done for so many of the people tonight.

As I endeavor to press through the multitude to reach the car, people are pushing and touching me while smiling and shouting. Many of them are trying to show me their miracle while others are touching me, hoping to be healed.

As we enter the vehicle and slowly maneuver the car amidst the throng, the people begin to disburse. It is as though a dam has burst as the people pour from the football field to go home. They are singing and praising God for what they have witnessed, overcome with a new love for this Jesus.

Yet I am informed that thousands of the people have refused to leave the field. They are saying, "No. We must stay here and wait for the woman of God who will come back tomorrow. Maybe her shadow will pass over us and we will also be healed. **She taught us that nothing is too hard for God!**"

As I hear these words, I remember the record in Scripture describing the ministries of the early Apostles of Jesus (Acts 5:15). Truly we are witnessing Bible days here in Kikwit.

By the time we arrive at our hotel, a large number of people have gathered to tell us about the miracles that they have seen.

The Town is Talking About Jesus

• Now two hours later, it is reported to us that thousands of the people have remained on the Festival grounds, refusing to leave.

• We receive another report of a blind woman who went home after the conclusion of the Festival without receiving her miracle, but when she arrived at her home, she suddenly received her sight. She used her cell phone to call one of her family members who was still at the Festival grounds to report her miracle. ...*And so it was that as she went* (home), *she was healed. And ...when she saw that she was healed,* (called back to the festival grounds), *and with a loud voice glorified God.* Lu.17:14-15 NKJV That wonderful news spread among the people who are still on the field. They are singing and rejoicing saying:

"This Jesus is the only great God! He opens blind eyes and heals cripples so they can walk! Hallelujah!

"Blessed are our eyes for the things that we are seeing. To God be the glory, for the Great things He has done!"

• The whole town is talking about this Jesus who performs miracles. Rain begins to fall and the people shout, "See the miracle of the rain, because the servant of God has come to Kikwit." (I was not aware that Kikwit had been suffering from a prolonged drought.)

Pastors Are Overwhelmed

Two of the pastors that invited me to Kikwit have come to my hotel room. They are completely overwhelmed by what they have seen.

• One remembered that when I first came to the Democratic Republic of the Congo last year I stated, "I am a sign and a wonder for you." He said, "Now we see it!"

• The other pastor remembers that during the Seminar I told them that, "Soon Kikwit will be known as the place of miracles in the Democratic Republic of the Congo."

• Another pastor from Kinshasa has come to Kikwit on personal business. He was informed that we are here, so he searches to find us. Just as he arrives at our hotel lobby, he observes us negotiating with the hotel manager for the needed gasoline to run the generators for additional days so that we might have electrical power to charge the batteries for our video camera and computers.

The Kinshasa pastor intervenes during the negotiations and generously offers to pay for the needed gasoline to run the generators for two hours daily during the next two days. We thank God for this miraculous provision. He knows our needs! The Scripture is proven again, ...*my God shall supply all your need according to His riches in glory by Christ Jesus.*[Phil.4:19 NKJV]

Osborn Ministry Fruit Continues

As I visit with this pastor, I learn

that he is a spiritual son of my father. He informs me that he never went to Bible School. His entire ministry training was received through my father's books that were distributed in the DRC many years prior. This pastor now has a vibrant ministry and is well known all across the nation.

In every country where I minister, men and women come to me who were launched into Gospel ministry by either the face-to-face witness of my parent's ministry, or through their books and teaching materials. It is truly amazing to learn about the global impact of the Osborn Ministries. As the Scripture has promised, so we are witnessing. *"For as the new heavens and the new earth Which I will make shall remain before Me," says the Lord, "So shall your seed and your name remain."* Isa.66:22 NJKV

The great harvest of our Gospel endeavors does not end. Jesus said, *You did not choose Me, but I chose you and ordained you that you should go and bear fruit, and that your fruit should remain.*

Jn.15:16NJKV When we minister to the people of a nation, in one way, we never leave. The seeds that we plant remain and continue producing ever-increasing harvests for generations.

At the close of the Day One meeting, thousands of people refuse to leave the field. They are saying, "No. We must stay here and wait for the woman of God who will come back tomorrow... She taught us that nothing is too hard for God!"

Three years ago, this woman fell and broke her arm and then broke her leg. On Day Two of the *Festival of Faith and Miracles*, she exclaims her healing before Dr. LaDonna and the Festival crowd.

This young woman had been paralyzed for five years. On Day Two of the *Festival of Faith and Miracles*, she raises her hands to show the people that she is completely delivered.

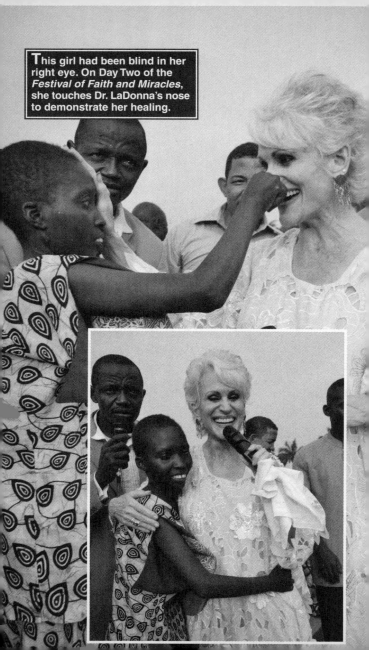

This girl had been blind in her right eye. On Day Two of the *Festival of Faith and Miracles*, she touches Dr. LaDonna's nose to demonstrate her healing.

Chapter 6

The Evangelism Festival Continues

As I PREPARE to leave the hotel for the Festival grounds, reports are coming in. So many people have already gathered there. They refused to go home last night.

Now I am told that they are smiling, singing and talking about what Jesus is doing.

Last evening was the largest public gathering in the history of Kikwit. The pastors are stunned, and they are shaking their heads in amazement. They know now that Jesus is ALIVE IN KIKWIT!

Even before the Festival begins on

this second day I know what is going to happen. The results are already stated in the Scripture. In God's mind the sick are already healed. The lost are already reconciled to Him. I just go in Jesus' name and pull back the curtain of Satan's lies so that the people may witness the victory that Christ has already won for all who believe.

Our confidence is firmly established in what Jesus has already accomplished at the cross and in who He has redeemed us to be. We are His Ambassadors of GOOD NEWS.

> **When we do what Christ commanded His followers to do,**
>
> **He will do what He promised to do.**

As I stand in the midst of this sea of men, women, young adults and children, I experience a renewed sense of *God's great love for people.*

• Why else would He send us so far to a place where no one has come before, to people whom by human standards have so little to offer?

• The only possible answer is **God's LOVE**—His divine, unconditional love. It is this love that guarantees our success here in Kikwit. Jesus is eager to show Himself to these hurting people, just as He has shown Himself to others.

As I arrive on the Festival grounds the people begin to shout and wave. There is great excitement in the air. I greet them and appeal to them to not push forward. I caution them about the sick people who are lying on the ground. It is precious to see how willing the people are to do everything that I ask. As the Festival begins, they cannot contain their joy as I reflect on the many miracles that were reported last evening.

Testimonies are still being reported

of people who were healed while they were on their way home last night.

When I ask the people how many of them did not attend yesterday's Festival service, it seems that 90% of the multitude raise their hands, indicating that they have come for the first time today. We will never know how many came yesterday, received their miracle from the Lord, and simply returned home.

Faith Is The Key

Tonight my topic is "Have Faith in God." I tell the people the story of the desperate father who brought his son to Jesus. I explain to them that the key to this story is the conversation between the father and Jesus. The father said to Jesus, "IF you can do anything, please help us." Jesus' answer teaches us how to receive from God today. He said, *IF YOU CAN BELIEVE...*[Mk.9:22-23 NKJV] These people understand the message.

I tell them:

> **"Your first step of faith
> is to believe in Jesus.**
>
> **"Your second step of faith
> is to accept His saving life.**

"When you do that, you give your-self completely to Him."

The people are so eager to take that first step. When I ask them who is ready to receive Jesus, a sea of more than 100,000 hands reaches toward the sky. This is a beautiful scene of one of the ripe fields that Jesus told us, are ...*ready for harvest.*[Jn.4:35 NKJV] The pastors continue to be amazed.

After the prayer to receive Christ, I give the new believers instructions on how to develop this wonderful new relationship with Jesus.

I am so thankful that we were able to give thousands of our book, 10 GOSPEL BASICS, to the pastors during the Seminar to assist them in disciplining these many new converts who will come into their churches. But the need for even more books is so great. We will print more of these valuable materials as God provides the funds through His people.

A Parade of Wonders

Now it's time to pray for the sick. I tell the people what God says to them through His words and promises:

*The Lord sends His word and heals YOU...*Psa.107:20 NKJV

*I am the Lord who heals YOU.*Ex.15:26 NKJV

*I am the Lord, I do not change...*Mal.3:6 NKJV

I am the Lord... Is there anything too hard for Me? Jer.32:27 NKJV

There has not failed one word of all (My) *good promises, which* (I have) *promised...* 1Kg.8:56 NKJV

...by (Christ's) *stripes YOU are healed.* Isa.53:5 NKJV

(I) *forgive all your iniquities,* (I) *heal all your diseases.*Psa.103:3 NKJV

Jesus went about…healing every sickness and every disease among the people. Mat.9:35 NKJV

Jesus Christ is the same yesterday, today, and forever. Heb.13:8 NKJV

Jesus…gave His disciples power over unclean spirits…to heal all kinds of sickness and all kinds of disease. Mat.10:1 NKJV

These signs will follow those who believe…they will lay hands on the sick, and they will recover. Mk.16:17-18 NKJV

Whatever you ask in My name, that I will do… Jn.14:13 NKJV

Everyone who asks receives… Mat.7:8NKJV

As I begin declaring those promises, people all across the Festival grounds begin to receive their miracles. Rather than interrupt this miracle atmosphere with a prayer, I simply announce that the people are healed in the name of Jesus, according to the Scripture.

There are pockets of eruptions throughout the field as people begin receiving their healing. Those who are near the people that have received their miracle, break out in shouts of joy and amazement.

I give the people instructions, pleading with them to not push forward, but rather to help those who have been healed to come to the platform so that they may testify. The people are trying their best to cooperate but it is nearly impossible for them to squelch their excitement and expectation.

Soon the platform is transformed into a *parade of wonders*, all wrought by the power of God, as the people believe on Him.

- Cripples are walking without their crutches.

- Many who were paralyzed or victims of accidents are rejoicing and demonstrating their healing.

- A deaf mute boy is healed, and

he clearly speaks the words of his own miracle testimony.

• Two blind children are healed; they are now seeing.

• An old blind man is waving his arms with excitement. He is seeing perfectly.

• A woman comes forward and tells us, "The woman of God said, 'If you had a tumor, look for it. It's gone.' I looked for the large tumor on my side, but I could not find it; it is gone!" Hallelujah!

• I am not sure that the people have heard this woman's wonderful testimony, because another former cripple is walking on the platform and the people are pointing and shouting for joy.

There are so many miracles happening, the people simply cannot focus on one testimony. This is truly the CHAOS OF MIRACLES. The resurrection life of Jesus is being evidenced here in Kikwit.

It will be impossible to hear all of the testimonies because of the late hour, so I request my interpreter to lead the people in a song of praise to God. The sound of the multitude singing

"Hallelujah" is certainly a preview of heaven, where the multitudes of people, from every kindred, tribe and tongue will gather around the throne. (Rev. 7:9-10)

Many of these beautiful Congolese from Kikwit will be there, BECAUSE, THANKS TO OUR PARTNERS, WE CAME. We thank God for allowing us to be His messengers of hope, peace and healing in a very forgotten place.

There are pockets of eruption throughout the field as people begin receiving their healing. Those who are near the people that have received their miracle, break out in shouts of joy and amazement.

There are so many miracles happening, the people simply cannot focus on one testimony. This is truly the CHAOS OF MIRACLES. The resurrection life of Jesus is being evidenced here in Kikwit.

Brought very far from another village, this child had never stood in his life. On Day Three of the *Festival of Faith and Miracles*, he is learning to walk for the first time, healed by God's miracle love-power.

Chapter 7

Miracles Attract
the Multitudes

THIS IS A new day. As we drive the 20-minutes from our hotel to the Festival grounds, we see people walking along both sides of the road, carrying their chairs or their sick.

They Come to Hear About Jesus

By the time we are one kilometer from the football field, both sides of the road has become a flowing river of people that are coming to hear about this man Jesus. I am told that some of these people have traveled for hundreds of kilometers to come to Kikwit to be healed.

As we begin the Festival service, I

ask the people who of them are here for the first time. Again, it seems that this is the first service for nearly the entire crowd. The multitude is enormous. I cannot see the edge of the crowd. At least 80,000, possibly as many as 100,000 people, are packed together on the football field all the way to the extreme sides in all directions.

Even the trees that surround the field are full of people. They are clinging to every branch all the way to the top, attempting to see what is happening among the people on the field and to hear the message of God's love for them. This is evangelism. This is why we have come.

The presence of the Lord is so strong in this place. The people are excited and they are ready to hear about Jesus. Their faith is filling the atmosphere.

Connecting People to Local Churches

Before I preach, I want the people

to meet the pastors who invited us to Kikwit. My work here is not complete until I have guided these people to the local churches.

I must also teach the pastors how to continue the Festival in the areas near their own churches. This kind of a spiritual visitation can continue for months, even years after we depart, if the pastors will encourage the evangelists to preach Jesus and to pray for the sick in the public places near their churches. This is soul-winning out where the people are. (See my father's book, SOULWINNING at www.osborn.org.)

The Power of Jesus

After we have introduced the pastors to the people, it is time to open the Word of God. The people become very calm and attentive. I tell them about the power of Jesus who delivered the woman in the Bible from the spirit of infirmity who had caused her to be bent over double for 18 years

(Lu.13:10-17). I teach them the lessons that we learn from this story.

- When Jesus called her, *she came*.
- When Jesus spoke to her, *she believed*.
- When Jesus touched her, *she was delivered*.

The living Jesus is still calling, speaking to and touching people today, whom Satan has bound. As the people grasp the implications of this message, they begin to shout with understanding and with faith.

The first step is for the people to *come* to Jesus. He is calling them. I ask who wants to come to Jesus, emphasizing that I am only praying for those who have *never* received Christ. The people insist that this is their FIRST time to receive Jesus into their own lives.

With great sincerity the multitude calls on Jesus. They receive His great and loving forgiveness. Then the people lift their hands saying, "Thank you, Jesus!" What a beautiful sight.

People Are Eager to See Jesus

Before praying for the sick I remind the people that when Jesus *spoke* to the woman in the story, she believed Him. Then I open my Bible and I read to them the words of Jesus concerning their healing, so that they can hear and believe His words.

> **When we announce God's promises, we are sending forth the healing life of God out among the people.**

As they begin to cry out to Jesus, I command the spirits of infirmity to leave the people.

• Before I can instruct those who were sick to begin acting their faith, crutches are being thrust into the air. Women and men are walking without their canes and walking aids.

Jesus is so eager to show His love to these people.

• One woman who has not been able to walk for 13 years, without a leg brace and two crutches, begins weeping, shouting and walking with ease.

• By now there are at least eight people on the platform who were crippled, and are now walking and demonstrating their miracle as the multitude shouts with excitement.

• A little boy is standing by me crying. He looks to be about four years old. His uncle has brought him from a village that was very far away. The boy has never been able to walk or support his weight on his legs. This beautiful child is now standing without any assistance, but he is quivering and looking so frightened. I carefully take his two little hands in mine and help him to walk, just like you would teach a baby to walk. He stops crying as he realizes that this new walking activity is fun. Then I release his hands and let him grab one of my fingers with one of his hands. Already he is walking confidently with very little help. Then he releases my finger and walks to his uncle without assistance. What a precious moment.

God's will is being done ON EARTH and the people are giving glory to Him.

• Several blind people are waving to the crowd and touching my nose, to prove that they can now see. The people laugh and they are over-joyed!

• The number of outstanding miracles is greater than we can document. All through the crowd there are outbursts of joyful shouts as miracles occur.

This is the CHAOS OF MIRACLES in Kikwit. It is impossible for all of those who have been healed to make their way to the platform to report their miracle. The people are simply packed too tightly together.

As the people rejoice, I encourage them to tell everyone what they have witnessed and what they have heard, as they go to their homes, reminding them to, *give thanks to the Lord! Call upon His name; Make known His deeds among the peoples! Sing to Him, sing psalms to Him; Talk of all His wondrous works!* 1Chr.16:8-9 NKJV The multitude begins singing for joy.

People Respond
When Jesus Passes Their Way

It is time for me to leave the platform. But my car has been moved. I cannot stay on the platform or the people will push forward until there is a stampede. If I stand by the road, the throng will crush me. There is no choice but to begin walking toward the road with the crowd.

Reverend Jackson presses forward ahead of me attempting to make a path for me through the people. Police and ushers are attempting to prevent the people from overtaking me. My clothing, my feet, my hands and my hair are being grabbed as people try to touch me. Their excitement cannot be contained as they shout and wave to me.

After about 15 minutes our car catches up with us. Reverend Harry and I pile into it, looking back in an effort to find the rest of our team. I spot my grandson Aaron, holding his camera over his head trying to capture this moment in photographs. Then I see Reverend Jennifer's head above the crowd as she presses through the people toward the car holding her video camera and tripod high in the air.

As Aaron scrambles into the car I say to him, "When you read in the Gospels about the multitudes who thronged Jesus, son, THIS IS A MULTITUDE! This is how *people respond when Jesus passes their way*. You are a blessed young man, to witness these events." Aaron will never forget this experience.

The Lord is doing great things in this place. The name of Jesus is being heard throughout the streets and in every home in Kikwit. This mission is making a difference that will last!

Most of the pastors here have never seen miracles. They are amazed and overjoyed by what they are witnessing. One pastor confesses to me, "I've preached about miracles, but I never believed in my heart that such things could happen. Now I see the power of God. Now I believe. Now I too will see miracles in my ministry."

Even the trees that surround the field are full of people. They are clinging to every branch, attempting to see what is happening among the people on the field and to hear the message of God's love for them. This is evangelism. This is why we have come.

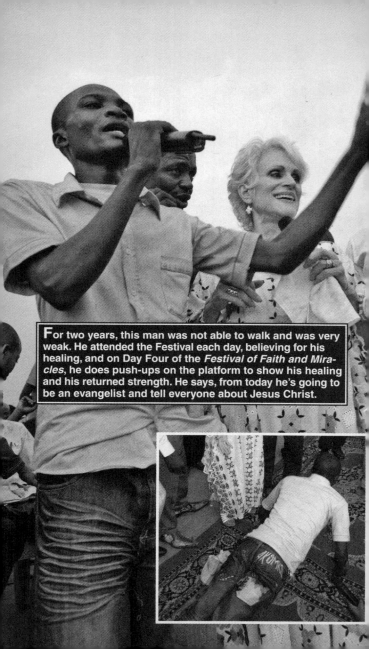

For two years, this man was not able to walk and was very weak. He attended the Festival each day, believing for his healing, and on Day Four of the *Festival of Faith and Miracles*, he does push-ups on the platform to show his healing and his returned strength. He says, from today he's going to be an evangelist and tell everyone about Jesus Christ.

Five years ago, this university student's back became so stiff and painful that he had to drop out of school. On Day Four of the *Festival of Faith and Miracles*, he is healed of the pain in his back and he demonstrates his new found flexibility.

This woman was bent over and walked using her hands (see inset), unable to stand up straight. On Day Four of the *Festival of Faith and Miracles*, she demonstrates her healing by walking hand in hand with Dr. LaDonna across the stage in triumphant celebration.

Chapter 8

God's Will in Heaven Comes to Earth

THE FINAL DAY of the *Festival of Faith and Miracles* is creating a great excitement here in Kikwit. People are coming from far away towns and villages to the football field because they yearn to experience the power of this great God.

It is a struggle for us to get to the platform because so many tens of thousands of people have already gathered. The platform is entirely encircled by the multitude. We are told that at least 100,000 people have pressed onto this field, desperate to receive relief from the sickness and torments of Satan.

The people welcome me with shouts and waves. All along the edge of the field, the trees are packed with people once again. They are all waving to me and shouting, "Welcome Woman of God!" I return the welcome, as I learn that once again nearly everyone in the crowd has come to the Festival for their first time.

In these evangelism events, we cannot take shortcuts. Each day must be approached as though it is the first day of the event, for indeed it is the first day, for most of the multitude.

Jesus Wants to Heal People

Today I help the people to know that Jesus WANTS to heal them. I tell them the story of the leper who came to Jesus (Mt. 8:1-3). The man was so hopeless and desperate, just like so many of the hundred thousand people who have gathered on this field. As I recount the Bible story, it seems that I can hear these dear Congolese people saying to Jesus the same words spoken by the leper, "If you want to, you can heal me." How quickly Jesus answers them, "YES, I WANT TO! BE HEALED!"

The compassion of Jesus has not changed. He is here in Kikwit, *eager to touch*, *to cleanse*, and *to heal* the broken lives that have come to Him.

Receiving Jesus
—A New Birthday—

I give special time to help the multitude of people receive Jesus and to understand the great new birth that they are experiencing.

Jesus said, YOU must be born again. Jn.3:7 NKJV

Whoever calls on the name of the Lord shall be saved. Ac.2:21 NKJV

The blood of Jesus Christ cleanses (YOU) from all sin. 1Jn.1:7 NKJV

Jesus said... I have come that YOU may have life... Jn.10:10 NKJV

Believe on the Lord Jesus Christ, and YOU will be saved... Ac.16:31

Even the little children are praying with great sincerity, asking Jesus to be their Savior. The multitude rejoices with great joy because they are now new creations and they have a NEW BIRTHDAY, for they are now truly BORN AGAIN!

A Field of Miracles

The people are eager for the healing prayer. I remind them that Jesus has power over every curse and every disease. Then I ask them to lay their hands on their own bodies, wherever they want Jesus to touch them. It seems that everyone is sick. I can hardly believe what I am seeing. Even children are holding their heads and praying for a miracle from Jesus.

After the prayer and the time of giving thanks, the people begin to act their faith. The entire multitude is a wave of motion as people begin bending their bodies, lifting their arms and moving their once crippled legs.

As the people begin to realize that they are healed, shouts can be heard throughout the crowd. Those who are being healed begin to move toward the platform, although I cannot imagine how any of them are able to navigate their way through the multitude that is packed so tightly together on these Festival grounds.

Today we are witnessing a great display of God's will to heal those whom Satan has tormented.

• One woman shows us the large callouses on her hands, where she had been crawling on her hands and knees for years, unable to raise up. Now she is perfectly healed, running and jumping for joy on the platform as she thanks Jesus for her miracle.

• A little six-year-old girl is walking for the first time in her life. She looks stunned as her mother rejoices.

• Another woman brings her son who had been a deaf mute. Yesterday his healing began and today he is listening to the radio and beginning to form words for the first time in his life.

• Another deaf mute who is completely healed makes it to the platform. This young man is speaking clearly as he testifies about his miracle to the people.

• Another man comes to tell us that a curse had been placed on him. One of his shins had two large sores that oozed constantly. He says that during the prayer the pain left his legs and the oozing stopped. The people are amazed to see this evidence of Christ's authority over the power of Satan.

• I have lost count of the number of blind people who are taking great delight in demonstrating their healing. The people celebrate with these who can now see.

• Several more cripples are abandoning their crutches and walking sticks, creating a new pile of discarded walking aids on the platform. Some of those who are healed are running and jumping as they celebrate their miracle.

There is such great joy in this place, the CHAOS OF MIRACLES continues.

• A woman testifies that she had been insane, or demon possessed, for the last five years. She smiles with contagious joy as she thanks Jesus for delivering her.

• Another young man comes to tell us that he has been sick for two years. He has been in the hospital and has undergone surgery but it didn't help him. He was forced to abandon his university studies. But now he is completely healed and to prove it, he drops down on the platform and begins to do pushups! He announces to the people that he will dedicate the rest of his life to telling people about Jesus. He says, "Jesus has healed me so I will be His evangelist to my entire province."

For nearly one hour we hear testimonies of people who have received a miracle from Christ. Of course I know that for every one who makes it to the platform, there are hundreds more who cannot come to tell us what they have received from Jesus. So great are the wonders of God in this place. I can only say what they said in Bible days, *We never saw anything like this!*
Mk.2:12

As we lead the people in a song of rejoicing, cloths and handkerchiefs are being waved all across this field of miracles. It seems as though no one has left the grounds, yet as we make our way to the hotel, both sides of the road have become a flow of people walking away from the field. They shout and wave to us as we drive by.

The Spirit of Evangelism Has Taken Hold

Kikwit will never be the same. To-morrow the churches will be packed with new believers, and next week in-spired evangelists and pastors will continue the Festival in every part of this city, preaching Jesus and allowing Him to demonstrate His love to the people through miracles.

As the Festival concludes, we can see that Kikwit will never be the same. Inspired evangelists and pastors will continue the Festival in every part of this city, preaching Jesus and allowing Him to demonstrate His love to the people through miracles.

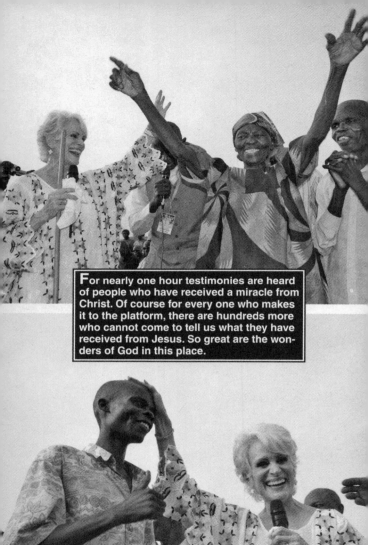

For nearly one hour testimonies are heard of people who have received a miracle from Christ. Of course for every one who makes it to the platform, there are hundreds more who cannot come to tell us what they have received from Jesus. So great are the wonders of God in this place.

In Kikwit, DRC as in every country where she ministers, men and women come to Dr. LaDonna who were launched into Gospel ministry by either the face-to-face witness of her parents' ministry, or through their books and teaching materials. It is truly amazing to learn about the global impact of the Osborn Ministries.

Chapter 9

Gospel Mission

AS THE WORK continues here in Kikwit, our team prepares to make the 10 to 12 hour road trip to Kinshasa from where we will begin our homeward journey.

Our sights are already set on the next mission. As Jesus said, *Let us go into the next towns, that I may preach there also...*Mk.1:38 NKJV

The Global Fields
Are Ready to Harvest

It is time to start the presses rolling to print thousands of more gospel books that we will distribute during our next mission. Each new outreach requires faith, as we trust God to provide the funds through His people.

The actions and influence of this ministry are at work every hour of every day. Even as we are involved in face-to-face ministry on one front, our materials such as books, DVDs and teaching courses are at work proclaiming the GOOD NEWS of Christ on many more fronts in nations worldwide. Plus the impact of this global ministry *continues* through the thousands of soulwinners that we have trained during our *Gospel Seminars*, and through the new ministries that are launched after our evangelism Festivals.

If we had one million dollars today, we would invest every penny in these effective, Bible-based actions to bring Christ to hurting people. What we do works! And the seeds continue to produce great harvests.

Jesus said, *The harvest truly is plentiful...*Mt.9:37 NKJV and indeed it is.

Before we leave Kikwit, certain individuals are coming both for prayer and to give us additional praise reports. It is thrilling to see what happens in cities like this when Jesus is able to show His love and power to the people. Faith has been activated in their hearts and the fruit of what has begun here will continue for generations to come!

• One pastor from another country who was with us during all of the Kikwit events says to me, "I came to learn, and what I have seen will last me a lifetime. I have seen great wisdom and amazing faith. I have seen Bible-day ministry. I feel as though I have been with Jesus as He ministered to the multitudes."

• I meet with the Organizing Committee to give them final guidelines concerning how to trust God and how to experience His miracle demonstration in their own ministries. They are so happy for this great visitation of God to their town. They are committed to continuing the miracle ministry of Christ here, working together just as they have during our gospel events.

• A Catholic sister comes to tell us that she is going to partner with one of the local pastors, to support the work of evangelism in this area.

• Another young man tells us that he is an evangelist and now he knows how to win people to Jesus. He says, "I am beginning immediately to do what I have seen you do!" I encourage him with these words, "Preach Jesus; pray for the sick; have faith in God; and don't end any evangelistic meeting until miracles of healing are witnessed! Jesus always wants to show His love for people."

This is Bible day evangelism!

We have shared with you what God has wrought here in Kikwit, DRC.

Christ's LOVE and POWER have produced a CHAOS OF MIRACLES that will long be remembered in this region. Join us as we *give thanks to the Lord! ...Make known His deeds among the peoples! Sing to Him, sing psalms to Him; Talk of all His wondrous works!*1Chr.16:8-9 NKJV

Christ's Unchanging Ministry

Now after more than six decades of mass miracle evangelism we are witnesses that the LOVE and POWER of Jesus has not changed. Everywhere that we carry His GOOD NEWS, Christ's healing presence gives testimony to His resurrection LIFE.

We are pressing into yet new and unreached areas with the Gospel of Christ. In every nation, in each city, during all of our public evangelism *Festivals of Faith and Miracles*, tens of thousands of people accept Christ as Savior and thousands of men and women experience His healing power.

In more than 100 nations, we are on the go, proclaiming and demonstrating the *resurrection life of Jesus Christ*, available to **all** who believe on Him.

What God has done among the people of Kikwit is His desire to do in every town.

Let's continue running with the message of GOOD NEWS to ALL people everywhere. As we each do our part, a great soul-harvest is reaped in every nation.

Bible Days Are NOW

As this book goes to press, *Jesus Christ* [is still] *the same yesterday, today, and forever.*[Heb.13:8 NKJV] What *He began both to do and teach*[Ac.1:1NKJV] throughout Galilee, He *continues to do and teach* through believers in this 21st Century.

In each nation where we minister, *Great multitudes follow Jesus, because they see His signs which He performs on those who were diseased.*[Jn.6:2 NKJV]

With great power (we are giving)... witness to the resurrection of the Lord Jesus. And great grace is upon us all.^{Ac.} 4:33 NKJV

Many signs and wonders are being done among the people. And believers are being increasingly added to the Lord, multitudes of both men and women.^{Ac.5:12,14} NKJV

God also bearing (us) witness both with signs and wonders, with various miracles, and gifts of the Holy Spirit.^{Heb.2:4} NKJV

Share this book with your friends. Order extra copies so others will know what God is doing through this global ministry.

- You are a part of all we do.
- You go with us through your partnership.
- You reap every harvest with us.

And God is able to make all grace abound toward you, that you, always having all sufficiency in all things, may

have an abundance for every good work.
2Cor.9:8 NKJV

We then (you and us), *are workers together with Him...*2Cor.6:1 NKJV

"In more than 100 nations, we are on the go, proclaiming and demonstrating the *resurrection life of Jesus Christ*, available to all who believe on Him."
– Dr. LaDonna C. Osborn and Dr. T.L. Osborn

OSBORN MINISTRIES -

- Angola
- Argentina
- Armenia
- Australia
- Austria
- Azerbaijan
- Bangladesh
- Belarus
- Belgium
- Benin
- Bermuda
- Bolivia
- Botswana
- Brazil
- Bulgaria
- Burkina Faso
- Burundi

- Cambodia
- Cameroon
- Canada
- Central Afr. Rep.
- Chad
- Chile
- China
- Colombia
- Congo (Dem. Rep.)
- Congo (Rep.)
- Costa Rica
- Cuba
- Denmark
- Dominican Rep.
- Ecuador
- Egypt
- El Salvador
- England
- Estonia
- Ethiopia
- Finland
- France
- Gabon
- Georgia

- Germany
- Ghana
- Grand Bahama
- Guatemala
- Haiti
- Honduras

LEGEND

Nations in which the Osborns have proclaimed the Gospel in face-to-face ministry.

- Hong Kong
- India
- Indonesia
- Ireland
- Italy
- Ivory Coast
- Jamaica
- Japan
- Kazakhstan
- Kenya
- Kyrgyzstan
- Laos
- Liberia
- Lithuania
- Luxemborg
- Madagascar
- Malawi
- Malaysia
- Mexico
- Mongolia
- Myanmar (Burma)
- Netherlands

- New Zealand
- Nicaragua
- Nigeria
- Norway
- Pakistan
- Panama
- Papua N.Guinea
- Paraguay
- Peru
- Philippines
- Poland
- Portugal
- Puerto Rico
- Russia
- Rwanda

- Senegal
- South Africa
- South Korea
- Spain
- Sri Lanka
- Sweden
- Switzerland
- Taiwan
- Tajikistan
- Tanzania
- Thailand
- Togo
- Trinidad
- Udmurtia
- Uganda
- Ukraine
- United States
- Uruguay
- Uzbekistan
- Venezuela
- Vietnam
- Virgin Islands
- Zambia

GLOBAL PUBLISHER

OSBORN INTERNATIONAL
P.O. Box 10
Tulsa, OK 74102 USA

❖❖❖

FRENCH DISTRIBUTOR

POSITIVE CONNEXION
BP 2072
51073 Reims Cedex, France

❖❖❖

GERMAN PUBLISHER

SHALOM — VERLAG
Pachlinger Strrasse 10
D-93486 Runding, CHAM, Germany

❖❖❖

PORTUGUESE PUBLISHER

GRACA EDITORIAL
Caixa Postal 1815
Rio de Janiero–RJ–20001, Brazil

❖❖❖

SPANISH PUBLISHER

LIBROS DESAFIO, Apdo. 29724
Bogota, Colombia

(For Quantity Orders, Request Discount Prices.)

www.OSBORN.ORG